Dream GIRL

A Young Woman's Guide to
PURPOSE, PASSION & TRUE SUCCESS

KEDIESHA R. WATKIS

Foreword by Kadian N. Walters, PhD

Destiny
BOOKS

———————————

Group Ordering Information:
Special discounts are available on quantity purchases by youth ministries, young women's groups, associations, and others.
For details, please contact
thedreamgirlmovement@gmail.com

Website: www.dreamgirlmovement.com

ISBN: 978-0-692-75483-2

Printed in the United States of America
First Edition

Edited by Kyshuri Ranger
Cover Design by Rounica White

He hath made everything beautiful in its season.
Ecclesiastes 3:12

~

To the memories of my late grandparents,
Dorrel Morgan and Violet Brown
who both were always very proud of all my achievements.

And to a group of young women whom I believe God has
entrusted me with- to see to their well-being, for whom I
foresee great things: Shanice Watkis, Savrenee Lee, Deborah
Simmonds and Adriel Miller,
may you be inspired to pursue your God-given dreams and live
purpose-filled lives to your fullest potential.

CONTENTS

Foreword by Dr. Kadian N. Walters

"Whatever you want to do, if you want to be great at it, you have to love it and be able to make sacrifices for it." These words from Maya Angelou epitomize Kediesha's story in her book **Dream GIRL**. I met Ked, as she is affectionately called, about ten years ago, at the annual Christmas banquet for Miracle Open Bible Church's youth group. Since then, our relationship developed as we worked together in the leadership of the Overcomers' Youth Department for several years. I have always admired her leadership style and how, despite adversities, she managed to 'stay on top of things'. When a dear friend in media asked me to recommend a young talent to work as her production assistant, I instantly thought of Kediesha!

Dream GIRL presents a realistic description of the highs and lows to be encountered on the journey to achieve one's dreams. It's very interactive, as it offers readers the opportunity to reflect on their own aspirations. The piece is timely, as today we live in a world in which many expect to accomplish their goals as soon as they start pursuing them. Many are seeking instant gratification, fuelled by social media networks such as Facebook and Instagram, where everything is shared in real-time. Unfortunately, this perfectionist view of life often leaves one disappointed. Such a microwave mentality has resulted in many deferred dreams, many buried goals and many dimmed visions.

As a university lecturer, I have seen some students, most of which are females, drop out of their programmes because of varying problems. I have also seen many, who with a little motivation, persevered to the end and emerged victorious in their endeavours. With scriptural insights, Kediesha provides the kind of motivation one needs to remain on course despite the challenges.

Young lady, what have you always dreamt of doing with your life? What is your dream profession? Do you lack the inspiration you need to move forward? Well, **Dream GIRL** is a powerful resource to help you on your way. The first part of this book gets you pumped up in *Gaining Inspiration* which motivates you to get going. You are encouraged to follow this up by *Releasing Limitations* and breaking all the chains that have had you bound, in the second section. If you are a parent or relative of a promising teenage girl you need to get her this book. If you are at a roadblock where nothing seems to be working in your favour, this book is also for you.

No stranger to failure and hardships, Kediesha offers readers insight into a journey of struggle and perseverance. In a world where the obstacles not only come from external forces but also from within one's mind, Kediesha reminds us that failure is not final. With only ten (10) chapters, it's an easy read, written in a conversational, matter of fact tone to motivate, uplift and inspire.

Who better to encourage young girls than one who has led and mentored other young ladies? For several years, Kediesha served as the president of our local church's Visionettes group, which caters to the social and spiritual development of teenage girls. Some of these girls have gone on to become promising young leaders as well. The holder of an honours degree in Literatures in English from the University of the West Indies, Kediesha showcases her talent and opens her heart in these pages, demonstrating how you can overcome adversities to accomplish your life's dreams. As the little girl with big dreams becomes one of the leading voices in Christian radio, she continues to excel. Now a graduate student in Media Arts at the Long Island University, New York, she continues to inspire and motivate those she comes in contact with. What a great inspirational tool for all of us who dare to dream!

Kadian N.Walters, PhD
Lecturer of Linguistics & Communications Consultant

A WORD FROM THE AUTHOR

Hi there! I'm so delighted that you have come across my book **Dream GIRL**. If you haven't purchased it as yet, I encourage you to do so now. You won't regret it! This book contains a wealth of wisdom which I've learned as a young woman in Christ, who dared to make her dreams come true. I wrote it so that other young women, from teen to adult, could be inspired to do the great things they desire, no matter their backgrounds, setbacks or circumstances. I also wrote it to document the wonderful things God has done in my life, and to celebrate what faith in Him can do.

Your Journey With This Book

Today many young women find themselves discouraged about life. Personal setbacks, financial difficulties, feelings of mediocrity, or even a negative environment have made them either give up the dreams they once held, or caused them to be nonchalant about the outcomes. If this describes you, I'm here to tell you that *your story can change*! You can live the dreams you've had, and I want to help you do so. Though technology has made it quite easy to access various kinds of self-help information, it's still priceless to have someone hold your hand and walk you through the important parts of life. If you don't have someone like that, I'm happy to take the position. If you already do, that's wonderful and I'm enthused to support your journey!

Dream GIRL will help you become inspired and excited about your dreams; it will put you on the path to making them reality. I encourage you to read this book in its entirety, and as you do, determine to use the lessons as stepping stones. Whatever it is that you're dreaming of, you can do it- get that degree, become the next great athlete, earn that scholarship, start your own business, become the leader you envision!

The book is divided into two parts- *Part One: Gaining Inspiration* and *Part Two: Releasing Limitations*. These section headings represent the main themes explored in this book. It should be easy for you to recall them, since the first letters when put together spell *GIRL*! At the end of each chapter is a *Dream Girl Reflection Section* for your own note-taking. This will help guide your thoughts as you read. Following this you will find another section called *Talking to God About…* This is a short prayer which may be used as you reflect on having your dreams come true. For me, prayer has been an important part in this journey and I want to share that with you.

If you're a parent or guardian, this book makes a great gift for your daughter, or that special young woman in your life whom you're grooming for success. Think of it as an investment in her dreams- the ones you already know will become true.

Finally, to you the reader, thank you for joining me on this journey. I hope this book touches you in a life-changing way!

they are from a particular background, they cannot dream in a particular way or they will never achieve what they have dreamed. **Dream GIRL** is a reminder to all of us, for I believe us older woman have all been to this place, and those coming will have experiences of this same thing- to be steadfast, keeping our eyes on our dreams and never to relent until we achieve them."

Danene Cruickshank,
Educator and Miss St. Catherine Festival Queen 2014,
Jamaica

"I read this book in only a few hours as it was engaging and came across as a thought riveting fire side conversation. Written with engaging stories, Kediesha reminds readers that one bad life circumstance does not mean that your dream or story is over. This book provides a person searching for a sense of purpose with answers, and a strategy for accomplishing their goals. This book is that little light that we all need at different intervals along the seemingly dim journey of life. In **Dream GIRL**, Kediesha shows us how to unearth our dreams, strategize and stay the course to achieving our dreams. Truly a landmark and relevant book with thought provoking principles to reenergize the reader toward the achievement of their dreams."

Odette Baugh,
Human Resources Professional

Dream GIRL

PART ONE

GAINING INSPIRATION

~

Your dream is a priority. And if it is a priority,
you must be intentional about investing in what
it takes to bring that dream to life.

~

Valorie Burton

1

Know That You Can Dream

Every girl has a dream, something she deeply desires to accomplish. Gone are the days when a woman could only aspire to become a wife, mother or home-maker. Although these remain noble choices, in this age, there are hardly any boundaries of what she may become. Women have now moved into every possible sphere of influence, and it all begins with having a dream. Often dreams arise from watching a role model, parent, celebrity or someone else with influence achieve something of great value. Dreams may also come from a lack of positive contributions in our environments, and this stirs a desire to be that person who makes a difference in our families, communities or the world at large. I've had dreams all my life. In fact, I can remember those I had at the tender age of eight. The biggest was to be a singer. I loved music and wanted to express myself through it. Besides, I believed I had a great voice (as others told me) and wanted the rest of the world to hear it. By the time I reached ten or so, my dream was to be a lawyer. Then by age eleven a writer, teacher, nurse, television or radio presenter and the list went on!

Upon completing university at age twenty, I became a step closer to making one of these dreams a reality (although by this time, most of my dreams had changed quite significantly, and some from childhood were crossed off my list!). Even though dreams may change, they give us something to look forward to. When I look back at some of those dreams, I often laugh- what was I thinking to want to do that?! Other times I wondered, what would have happened if life turned out that way instead?

The great thing about where I am today, is that many of my experiences and accomplishments did begin with a dream. They certainly did not all work in the exact ways planned, but I still got to many of the places imagined as I had conceived them. Allow me to share with you the journey of how that happened.

Early Stages

I've always dreamed of becoming a Journalist or another prolific person who practised media. From a very young age I pictured myself reading the news on a local radio or television station. As a child I was encouraged to watch the news and like many Jamaican families at that time, my family gathered in the living room at seven pm sharp every night to view the news. When it was over by eight pm, we turned to another TV station, again to watch the news. I could name all the television news presenters of the day. My favourites were Kerlyn Brown, Carol Francis and Dahlia Harris. I had similar interactions with the radio personalities. I literally grew up with the radios in my home stuck on two frequencies. On waking up and preparing for school, the voices of Allan Magnus and Dorraine Samuels would be heard in the background.

On some mornings it was Francois St. Juste. I loved to hear Francois bellow on the top of his lungs "Gooooood moorrrrning Jaaaaaamaaaaaicaaaaa". It was exciting! It was a thrill! I also enjoyed the on-going banter between the popular pair, Allan and Dorraine. I loved their voices– how eloquently they spoke, and the energy which emanated from them. This admiration continued for years, even today. By the time I got to the sixth grade level, my heart was set on a certain dream. I'd become a Journalist, reading the news on a local television or radio station. If I wasn't a news anchor, I'd be the weather reporter advising the nation about the impending conditions. This dream was often played out in class presentations when asked to talk about what I'd like to become when I grow up.

I have a vivid memory etched in my mind of how my dream grew inside my heart; again this was in the sixth grade. Being an avid reader I never missed reading *The Children's Own*– a local publication sold especially to school-aged children. I read other local publications too such as *The Star, Jamaica Gleaner* and *The Jamaica Observer*. Yes I read them all at the tender age of eleven. I remember coming across a spread in one of these papers– it may have been *The Children's Own*. The spread was a highlight of a well-known media house celebrating its 50th anniversary. It tracked how the radio station came into being and showed important transitions which took place over the period. My dream came alive even more as I viewed the pages with awe and deep interest.

On another occasion, still in the sixth grade my teacher told me I'd become like the veteran Broadcaster Ms. Fae Ellington. I liked the idea! In fact, I remember doing a quiz from *The Children's Own* which sought to match children with career fields and famous Jamaicans who worked in them. Believe it or not Ms. Ellington was one of those famous Jamaicans featured in the quiz. When I completed it my results matched me with her as well as the Linguistics and Broadcasting fields.

I carried my dream with me into high school. I will admit however, that there were numerous changes in mind about what I'd become. Still the dream did not die. In the ninth grade I simulated a newscast for a project in which I was International Journalist Katie Couric, and in the eleventh grade I was part of my school's short-lived radio club. That latter experience cemented my dream even further. That moment when I spoke over the school's intercom and heard my heart in my voice.... I knew there was a passion within me for something great.

We Give Life to Our Dreams

There's something really funny about dreams. They have their own life cycle. In fact, think of dreaming like breathing, every living human being breathes, naturally. So too, every human being dreams naturally, as there is an innate desire within to make something of our lives. When born in our minds, dreams grow as we think on them consistently. We can throw out some dreams (let's say we realise that's really not what we want), expand some, and even birth new ones at any given time or place. In their initial stages, we really don't need to do much for our dreams to survive. Just thinking about them will ensure they're kept alive. Again, I use the human analogy- at the most basic level, we can function as human beings once breathing. However, as we grow day to day, our body relies on other elements like water, food, exercise and so on for support. Dreams take on a similar behaviour. Like our bodies, they begin to place demands upon us and before long need more than mere day to day thinking for survival. Like babies they require increasing attention. This is where the rubber meets the road. For their fulfilment, our dreams require planning, resources, and most definitely *ACTION*. If ignored and starved of these important elements, they have the potential to die.

Write It Down

Where do you see yourself in five to ten years? I'm sure you may have pondered this question many times before, especially if you're a teen or young adult. Go ahead and think about it again for a few minutes. It is important that you realise you're neither too young nor too old to begin crafting a picture of your future life. In fact, I've found you are most likely to stay focused on your dreams when you write down exactly what they are. One beloved bible verse which supports doing this is Habakkuk 2: 2 which says:

"Write the vision and make it plain on tablets, that he may run who reads it. For the vision is yet for an appointed time; but at the end it will speak and it will not lie. Though it tarries, wait for it; because it will surely come, it will not tarry."

This verse has been a part of my life since about age seventeen, when like many teens I was uncertain about the direction of my life. It has provided me with comfort on so many levels and I want to share that with you.

"...Write the vision ..."

At varying intervals of life, I've written down what I wanted to accomplish. Whether it was a major or minor desire, I wrote it down. Even as I'm writing this book I have three lists of 'dreams to accomplish' which I revisit from time to time. Each list was made during very different points of my life but collectively they make up the overall direction for which I've aimed. One list makes me smile each time I read it because over the four-year period since it was written, a number of accomplishments really came through. At the time of writing them down I did not necessarily know exactly how they would be fulfilled. All I knew was they were what I wanted. My heart is warmed

27

when I look back on them. Those which have been fully accomplished I place a tick beside. If I'm not quite 'there' as yet, I scribble a note to document how far along the process is, and what else needs to be done.

Whatever age you are at right now- be it ten or twenty years old, know that your dreams are important. Write them down, even if you don't have a fool-proof plan of how to get to them.

---

*you're neither too
young nor too old
to begin crafting a
picture of your future
life.
Know that your
dreams are important*

Write them down and read them often. Make decisions in line with them. Make time to go after them. Share them with the important people in your life. Prepare yourself to pursue them. Look out for opportunities to fulfil them. Be ready when it's time to step into them.

"...the vision is yet for an appointed time...wait for it..."

While embracing your dreams and making plans in line with them, it is also important to recognise that timing is everything. Of course we all wouldn't mind our dreams coming through within a split second; but the truth is as mentioned in this verse - there is an appointed time. That's why you have to be ready when the time comes. That means there must be some period of preparation before launching out into your destiny, and each time you make a move toward the direction of your dream, you become one step closer to it. Be mindful though, one step closer to the appointed time can also mean setbacks. They are only part of the journey, so do not be disappointed when time goes by and life is not as you imagined.

For me, I've noticed that just before realising a dream, I usually experience a season of difficulties or disappointments on varying levels. Over the course of time however, I came to see that those were just 'waiting times'. I was sitting inside a waiting room. We each have them and they serve to prepare us for what is to come. On the journey toward success, this is a key piece of life's puzzle which we must understand. Often, the euphoria associated with pursuing our dreams clouds our minds and we tend to forget that we won't see the fulfilment of every dream all at once. The waiting room prepares us for what is to come, often processing those areas of our ability and maturity, which must be effective in the phase ahead.

If you are at a place of difficulty and disappointment, I encourage you to continue working toward your dreams. Whatever you're aiming for is achievable, and one day the appointed time will come. Eventually, we come out of our waiting room experience.

Begin Where You Are

My journey to accomplishing various dreams has been quite interesting. As I grew older, the direction for my life became much clearer and more defined. Mind you, there were certainly periods in which things were fuzzy. Upon entering high school, my biggest dream was to finish successfully and move on to getting a degree at a reputable university. Attending university was something no one in my immediate family had achieved. To do so would make them very proud and I wanted that. This dream required my complete focus, even in the midst of having my mother living in another country, and later learning she was diagnosed with cancer. Despite the challenges, I was undeterred. Sure enough, I ended high school on a good note. Disappointment however knocked on my door when I was not accepted into a formal pre-university (the coveted sixth form or senior class) programme. This was one of the lowest points of my teen years. I felt as if my achievement was not good enough. "This does not fit into the dream" I said. It wasn't part of the plan. Moreover, what would all my friends think? Birds of a feather huh? Somehow I started to feel as though I were never as brilliant as I thought. I never imagined taking an unplanned alternate route toward the next phase of my life. Having been rejected by other programmes, I felt awful. Both my grades and my behaviour were commendable,so why was this happening? "I am a smart girl! There must be some mistake", I thought. This was never in my dream.

It took quite some time for me to get out of the mental ditch I had placed myself in and see that my dream wasn't being denied. I just had to take another route. This other route was a private institution, away from most of my friends. Away from the prestigious high school which beamed with excellence, and from where I imagined I'd transition into my university years. I was less than enthused at the prospect of enrolling into this new school but it seemed worth a try. Putting away my gnawing feelings of inferiority, I settled within myself that excellence would remain my goal. Here I drew myself up by the bootstraps and propelled myself into a degree programme at the University of the West Indies- an achievement which took place within one year. The traditional route would have taken me two years. This was obviously my blessing disguised. Sometimes blessings seem like curses…the difference requires perspective.

The Time is Now

Nobody ever said making your dreams come true would be easy, but the exciting news is- you can begin where you are. Right now in your life you can start with a dream. What do you dream of achieving?

---

*For their fulfilment,
our dreams require
planning, resources, and
most
definitely ACTION*

What do you deeply desire to accomplish? I wish to challenge you this moment to *GIVE LIFE TO YOUR DREAMS*. Move them from the thought level to action. Begin planning the steps toward the next phase of your life, and even beyond. Map out what you will need for this journey and get ready for the drive. Remember now, you may experience a bump or two in the road but once you get pass them, press full speed ahead into your destiny. Pursue your dream with passion, and be persistent. Know that success is waiting for you!

Dream Girl Reflection Section

* What are some of the dreams you've had for your life?

*Describe the dream(s) you are now working towards or desire to fulfil.

*List three actions which can help you get there (for example going to college, joining a programme etc.)

* Write a vision for the life you wish to have.

Talking to God About - My Dreams

Prayer 1

Lord, I thank You for creating me with the ability to set goals, and to dream. I know that through Your strength, I can do all things (Phil. 4:13). I bring to You now the vision I have written down for goals I desire to accomplish. Increase my faith so that I may believe they will come to pass. Lord, I know it's important for me not only to believe, but to act also (Ja. 2:14). Grant me wisdom to know which action(s) to take, in order that I may be prepared to pursue my dreams. I thank You for what You are going to do in my life. Amen

2

Finding Your Strength(s)

In our youthful years, we're especially encouraged to try as many new hobbies or interests as possible. This is good advice that's certain to bring about skill development, discipline and hopefully fulfilment. But I must give you a word of caution - it will do a world of good once you understand it. Here goes: You won't be good or excellent at everything you try your hand at. Did I just say that? Yes I did! And I'm happy to say it again - You won't be good or excellent at everything you try your hand at. And guess what? There is no need to be! We are each equipped with talents through which we are destined to succeed- some we may be good at for a season, others for a lifetime. What is important is that you find the skill(s) or talent(s) which makes up your greatest strength(s). This is where you will unlock ultimate fulfilment and true success. Trust me, I know this very well!

Throughout my years in school, I found that I was always successful at the arts (subjects such as English Language, History, Literature etc.). My best friends however were really good at technical subjects and the sciences. They always solved the hardest mathematical problems and found joy in working out scientific formulae. I was quite the opposite. In high school math was my least favourite subject. While I consistently aced the arts, I struggled with math throughout the ninth grade and beyond. At times I felt really low about my aptitude in the subject- it just wasn't 'my thing'. I worked hard at pulling up my grades but they were never fantastic. Only after completing high school and getting ready to start university, did I truly learn to appreciate that my strengths were in the arts. In fact, I remember that while my friends solved their math problems, I read tonnes of books with ease. During the summer holidays all my literature books were read, so when school began I was reading them for the second time. They always marvelled at how I did this. And guess what? For some of them, reading like I did, was never in their favour.

One humorous memory I can recall on this topic is that,

during my last year of high school a classmate of mine was very fervent in advancing the idea that I would become a Librarian, based on my love for books and reading. It became his personal campaign of how he imagined me in the future.

---

find the skills

or talents

which make up your

greatest strength.

This is where you will

unlock ultimate fulfilment

and true success

When I started my first degree studying Literatures in English and History, I found there was so much which I knew in these areas from high school that was benefiting me at that level. It was never hard to read four or five books within eight to twelve weeks because I had already developed the love for critical reading and found it to be no burden. I am telling you this to show that it is ok to be average, or even less than stellar at some things. Never mind that, because there are other areas in which you will excel. You are no underachiever as a result of this. Take note that I am not saying you should throw in the towel once you're not good at something. What I am saying is, be mindful that as human beings we are all gifted at varying levels, and no one is excellent in every area! No one!

Be Yourself

I believe one of the greatest injustices someone can ever commit in this life, is attempting to be what they are not. Think about that for a moment. When you pretend to be someone you are not, you rob the world of your true value. Moreover, you rob yourself the opportunity to unearth the potential in you. That's why it's important for you to find your strength- that gift or talent which causes you to feel valued. We all possess them and once tapped into, our lives become much more productive and satisfying, so we won't feel the need to copy anyone else. In his books on strengths-based management and leadership, bestselling author, and motivational speaker Marcus Buckingham, says there are four clues which help point an individual to their strengths. Here's a brief summary of those clues:

* **It's not just what you're good at; but each time you do it, you feel effective.**

* **It's something you are naturally inquisitive**

about. You look forward to doing it.

•*You keep learning and researching about it.*

•*It reveals the best in you!*

The most important thing to note about these four clues is that the focus is on what you are most effective at! So many times we back-pedal on our dreams by focusing on an area in which we have trouble, as if life were some competition to determine how many things one can be great at all at once! On the contrary, it isn't. Stop placing too much attention on what you aren't passionate about, and more-so what is not critical for your success. Make a commitment to yourself today, to stop doing that. There is greater reward in investing your time and energy on things that really matter to your destiny. Again, this is not to be misunderstood as an excuse for mediocrity. There will be times in which we have to work on areas holding us back from a greater magnitude of success.

However you may view this thought, the truth is at any given time in life you grow the most in the areas you are strongest. Right now, can you identify those areas? Is it sports, business, culinary arts, performing arts, academics, cosmetology, home-making and decor? Whatever it is, I encourage you to deliberately seek out opportunities to use your strengths.

Develop Your Strengths

When you find your strength it is important that you take time to nurture it. This is the only way in which you'll be able to experience growth in that area. I've been a 'fan' of public speaking from a very early age. There was just something about standing on a platform and speaking before an audience that ignited and intrigued me. Truth be

---

seek out

opportunities

to use your strengths

---

told, throughout my years growing up I dreamed of one day becoming a motivational speaker. In fact, on tracing my development from childhood, I realise that I was often called upon to give speeches, votes of thanks, introduce guests, make presentations and so on. On any given occasion, I listened most keenly to those who spoke with passion, drive and sincerity. I was drawn by not just what they said, but how they said it.

By the time I entered high school, I knew public speaking was something I'd be good at. While I was aware of that fact,

I was never too sure how to get there. But one thing was for certain, I used my skill each time I got the opportunity.

My high school's Debate Society taught me much about the art of public speaking, and here my niche was further developed. Fast forward to my second year of university-the day I attended my first Toastmasters International meeting. This I remember quite well, because it left an indelible mark upon me. The posters advertising the club had caught my attention, and I entered the meeting just looking to see what it was all about. There was an activity called Table Topics which basically required you to think and speak 'on your feet' for approximately two minutes about a given topic. I can't remember volunteering; on the contrary I believe I was chosen at random to participate. Having no clue what this would all be about, I accepted the challenge. All participants were sent outside and one after the other we re-entered the room to learn our fate.

On my turn, I remember being totally relaxed and with my words commanded the attention of the entire room for the full two minutes. Where that came from, I don't know. I didn't plan it, but what came out of me was something great and when I was finished, the entire room knew this. That afternoon I won the award Best Table Topics Speaker. All the members of the club were quite impressed, and I remember being asked "have you done this before?" and "are you a trained speaker?", both to which I responded "no". "Did you debate in high school?", another person asked. "Well, yes" I said.

That afternoon changed my life in many ways. I realised that public speaking was not just something that I was good at- it was my strength. From then I started attending Toastmasters meetings every Thursday until I graduated university. After my first few meetings, I became a member (there was no escaping this- all the other members urged me to become a part of the club). Shortly after, I held a position on the executive body and for many meetings, often consecutively, retained the title Best Table Topics Speaker. Within a few months I started entering area and national contests- placing second and third respectively in one year. Later on, I started to mentor new members. Toastmasters became a solid part of my life. When I entered the world of work, employers and employees alike were impressed at my speaking and communication ability. Toastmasters followed me wherever I went.

After completing undegraduate studies, I continued attending meetings at other clubs and enthusiastically pursued the development of my strength. Because of my commitment to that task I have built a reputation for communicating well. This today continues to be one of my greatest personal and professional assets. I'm glad I was able to discover this as one of my strengths and push myself further into it.

As you are reading this, I encourage you to start thinking about your own gifts. Which talent of yours has brought you the most fulfilment, and can be marketed for your benefit and others? What do you need to do, in order to develop that particular thing? Does it require time and money? I challenge you to begin building yourself in that area today. Do not put it off for later in your life. Begin now!

Dream Girl Reflection Section

*What areas do you believe are your strengths?

*Describe how you feel when engaged in these activities?

*What steps will you take to invest in them?

Talking to God About - My Strengths

Prayer 2

Lord I recognize that You have created me with specific gifts and strengths (Ps. 139:14) which are connected to my purpose in life. Help me to discover these strengths and grant me the confidence and opportunities to use them. Show me where these strengths can be used to make a difference. Direct me on the path to developing them, not only to my benefit but for others (Matt.14: 19-23). Thank You for hearing my prayer. Amen

3

It's Alright to Fail

Earlier I mentioned that you will not be good at everything you try your hand at. In this chapter I'll unpack the thought further so that you understand it's alright to fail. Before I get deeper into the matter, let me hasten to say that this was not a lesson easily learned. As you can imagine, I had to fail at some things in order to truly understand what I'm about to tell you.

Failure is Never Final

At age twenty-two I began searching for a career path.

I was ready to pursue the skills which were my natural talents and passions, at all costs. I could not see any further progression in the job which I held at the time, and having gained considerable experience in the area thought it fit to move on. Thereon I was unemployed for nine months, during which time, I did considerable work in order to build myself for the media career I dreamed of. I boosted my communication and presentation skills by enrolling in a Speech certification course at which I was highly successful (most of my classmates wondered why I took the course in the first place...); I also explored the area of academic tutoring, which returned some success, so much so that I was armed with a business plan and in advanced preparation to begin offering formal classes. I sought numerous opportunities to put my skills to work.

When a friend of mine tipped me off on an opening at one of the most credible media houses in the country, I was on the moon, ready to give it my best shot. In no time, I submitted my application and was later called for interview. My big break was literally in my hands! I was on the verge of fulfilling my dream. On the day for the interview I looked my absolute best and was feeling very confident. I could not believe what was about to happen to me. Upon entering into the building, sensations of disbelief, joy and nervousness began flooding me even more. Since I was being interviewed for a News Presenter position, I voiced a demo news package. Later I was invited to a posh conference room, where my fate would be further determined. All eyes, approximately six pairs of them were on me as I gracefully and confidently answered each question. By the time it was over, I was naturally anxious, wondering of course, if I had made the cut.

The days which followed were quite agonizing as I awaited the call. At last, within a week or so my mind was put at ease. I still remember how my stomach churned listening keenly to the voice at the other end of the line. After confirming my name, my heart began doing back-flips. With my hopes as high as they could be I needed no cloud nine! Finally, my anxiety was eased, but my heart broke as I heard the words "I'm sorry you were not successful for the position." Once the call ended, hot tears ran down my cheeks, and a sea of emotions engulfed me. Anger, yes anger and disappointment. Anger, because I believed with all my heart that this was 'my big break'. I was angry at God, because He did not make this come through for me as I wanted, and disappointed because I was really hungry for the opportunity. I had always wanted to become a news reporter.

With my crushed heart I decided then that I would no longer pursue a media career. I gave up totally and put the dream aside- telling myself that I would never again apply for a media job because it was not what God wanted for me. If it was, He would have allowed me to get the job, I reasoned. This was a turning point in my life.

For seven months I stayed true to my words and became content with finding a job, any job. I applied for no media jobs. In fact, I explored other interests in the hope that they would lead me to success. This included graduate school. It was time for me to move on with my studies, I mused. After all, a Master's degree was another dream on my list. And thus I pursued, concluding that this must be what I should be doing with my life. In light of the fact that I was always a good student, I expected it to be a fulfilling journey.

Straighten Yourself, Move Forward

I was very proud of myself when I started a Master's programme. It was a task which I looked forward to. Being among other brilliant and ambitious professionals gave me a lot of confidence that I could be successful too. It gave me thrill and satisfaction. This was a new journey and I embraced it. Following the first few classes, things became challenging and exhausting. Relearning proper time management was a task all by itself. As we delved a little deeper into the courses I became disconnected from some, while drawing closer to others. For one particular course I was constantly behind, on account of missing two classes. I tried but never seemed to catch up. The reality that I'd

better buckle my seatbelt and focus on the journey came when I took a test for this course. I hardly understood what was before me but made an effort to complete the paper. I was growing pretty comfortable with the other courses, but this one rubbed me the wrong way. Weariness began setting in. Looking back, I can call it providence, but there was an incident which took place surrounding this course that I believed jolted me into the right direction. I am now happy I experienced it, but at the time, it left a bitter taste in my mouth.

One evening upon arriving home, I went to check my emails as I often did at that time. I noticed one from the lecturer of the course which was giving me a hard time. With much curiosity and tightness in my throat, I went ahead and opened it. It was a letter addressed to me and copied to the Head of Department, recommending that I be barred from taking the course's final exam. In addition, my lecturer expressed much disdain at my performance on the test. I had failed miserably.

*no circumstance in life
can eliminate you from
success,
unless you allow it*

Dismal- that's how I felt after reading the email, and I spent the night in tears, feeling like a complete failure. This was more than I could take. The days which followed found me in a sombre, reflective mood. I could not understand how I'd reached this point- nothing like this had ever happened to me before. My academic performance always meant much to me, and up to this point I was consistently an excellent student. How could this be? As the weeks progressed I continued with my classes and made great effort at giving it my best. The day came however when I realised I would not be fulfilled continuing the programme, so after heavy reflection I decided to withdraw entirely from it. It was a moment of complete honesty with myself. Yes, I had an interest in that Master's programme, however it was never my true dream. I was never genuinely connected with it. Instead, there was a desire within me to have something which I could show my family, friends and the world to say- "hey, I achieved this."

Deep inside of me was the desire to find the meaning and purpose of my life. Though I could have been successful at that, it was not the strength or move which would take me into the career of which I dreamed, so, like air which needed to escape my lungs, I let it go. Perhaps reading this, you are unable to understand my decisions. I've learned never to be content with the average or what will just get you by in life. Possibly, your own failures in life have been much more overwhelming than mine. It may have been a public embarrassment or something for which you now carry deep personal shame. I'd like you to know that no circumstance in life can eliminate you from success, unless you allow it. Hold on to this nugget of wisdom from Eleanor Roosevelt (First Lady of the United States, 1933-45) who once said- No one can make you feel inferior without your consent. Bear it in mind each time you are made to feel disqualified from the pursuit of your goals. Reach forward for your dreams, they are yours for the taking. From my own experience described in this chapter, I learned that my dreams meant something, and that they ought to be pursued with all that is within me. When I arrived at that conclusion, I did not have all the answers, but little did I know, I would soon find myself in the place of destiny.

Dream Girl Reflection Section

* What failures, if any, have you experienced while taking steps toward your dreams?

* How did you feel?

* What did others say to you about the experience(s)?

* How did you move pass them?

Talking to God About - My Failures

Prayer 3

Father, as I reach for my dreams, there are days when I feel as if I've failed. Sometimes I'm even angry at You for not bringing me into the kind of success I've expected. Lord, I've begun to see that one bad circumstance does not mean that my story will not end well.

I recognize too that You do not want me to succumb to feelings of discouragement, despair and failure (Psalm 42:5).

Rather, it is Your desire for me to be patient, while You're working things out for me. As I pursue my goals, help me to remember that You are with me. Remind me that Your desires for me are always good (Jer.29:11). Thank You Lord. Amen.

4

Purpose

Harlem

What happens to a dream deferred?
Does it dry up like a raisin in the sun?
Or fester like a sore
And then run?
Does it stink like rotten meat?
Or crust and sugar over like a syrupy sweet?
Maybe it just sags like a heavy load.
Or does it explode?

Langston Hughes

Since the time of the incidents from the last chapter, the biblical story of a young man named Joseph, has remained dear to me. It holds some important faith lessons which I hope never to let go of. While wondering what would be my next step, this story gave me hope. At a young age, Joseph recognised his gift- he was a dreamer, with the ability to interpret dreams. Being the zealous young man he was, when Joseph discovered this he shared it with his family- in fact he told them of a dream in which the sun, moon and stars bowed down to him. From there on Joseph's brothers became increasingly jealous of their sibling and devised a plot to get rid of him. They sold him into slavery and Joseph was taken into another land, Egypt. While in Egypt, Joseph found favour with a powerful man, Potiphar who put him in charge of all his affairs. Potiphar's wife became attracted to Joseph and constantly made attempts to seduce him. On one such occasion, Joseph refuses her advances and runs away from her. She then accuses him of forcing himself on her and Joseph is sent to prison.

While there Joseph meets two men- the cup-bearer to Pharaoh, king of Egypt, and his baker. One night, both men have troubling dreams. While sharing with Joseph they discover his gift and Joseph interprets the dreams for them. For the cup-bearer, his dream was good news. He would return to his position and again serve the Pharaoh. For the baker however, his dream actually foretold his death. Joseph's interpretations were indeed correct and in no time, the cup-bearer was on his way back to Pharaoh. On his departure from prison, Joseph tells the cup-bearer to remember him; however, it seemed he never did.

Two years elapsed and Joseph was still imprisoned. How agonizing that must have been? This young man had so much promise on his life. He held a dream in his heart, but there was no sign that it would ever be. What could have gone wrong? All he ever did was talk about his dream. I wonder if Joseph felt he was being punished. Isn't that how we feel at times? Our prayers have not been answered; our dreams are not working out as we planned; God must have forgotten us, we often say or think. Over the course of my young life, I've learned and continue to see that God's timing is nothing like ours. When we least expect it, He comes through on our behalf, showing that He really never did forget about us. He was only working things out for our good. And so it was with Joseph. After two whole years passed, Pharaoh, king of Egypt has a number of dreams which begin to trouble him. He seeks out his magicians and wise men, but none can interpret them. The cup-bearer finally remembers what happened to him in prison and tells Pharaoh about Joseph.

Without delay, Joseph finds himself before the king, who is anxious to hear what he has to say about the dreams. Like he did with the magicians and wise men, Pharaoh tells

Joseph his dreams and is astonished at the wisdom which flows from his mouth as he interprets them. This was the turning point in Joseph's life. Because of his wisdom and ability, the Pharaoh makes Joseph second in command in all of Egypt. Yes, Joseph is taken from prison to palace! Talk about a make-over and a half! I'm sure Joseph did not expect that he would have been sold into slavery by his own brothers, and later thrown into prison an innocent man before this great thing happened! There was a purpose on his life, and despite delays, it could not be thwarted.

Be Prepared for Your Destiny

I was at peace with my decision to withdraw from the Master's programme, but certainly anxious at what next would be. I had the task of discussing this with my parents. My greatest fear was that they'd think I was a failure. When we finally had the conversation, to my surprise they were fully understanding and supportive. That took a load off my shoulders. It was important to me that my parents supported me in my pursuits. On one occasion as I was having this talk with my mother, she shared with me her recollection of hearing that a Christian radio station which I listened to was seeking people to train and work with. It definitely piqued my interest and so I got all the information I could find online and gave them a call, along with sending an email. I learned that the radio station was about to launch a volunteer programme and needed persons to serve in various areas. Of course they highlighted that there was no guarantee of permanent employment. "An open door", I thought. Remember in the last chapter I mentioned not applying for any media-related jobs? Well, this was where that impasse ended. I put all my insecurities

---

a lack of immediate success or favourable results
does not mean you are on the wrong path

---

behind me, and got my documents ready for submission. Almost a month passed by before hearing any word on my application. By this time, I was really convinced that nothing would come of it. And then came the call for an interview. A glimmer of hope. On the morning of the interview, I awoke with a song in my heart. I felt that a change was coming. The day as I recall was December 20. The year was drawing to a close; for me it had proved to be a time of much praying, learning and waiting. There was a great desire for something new to happen in my life. I was happy to have made it through, being much wiser than at the start; I hoped that this was a favourable door about to be opened.

When the following year began I still did not know what was in store for me. As I did at the beginning of each new year, I was seeking the Lord for the direction of my life in prayer and fasting. My career was of course an area of focus as I sought Him. As I did so I prayed about the opportunity at the radio station, but was still remaining open to see if perhaps there was something different in store. At last, on one unsuspecting evening there came the anticipated call- I was selected for the programme and would begin that same week. The joy I felt on receiving that news could not be equated with another moment in those first few weeks of the new year. This was my Joseph experience. God did not forget about me! In fact, this was the beginning of a season of divine favour over my life.

Within a month of starting the volunteer programme, I was made a full-time offer to become the station's News Editor. In just another few months I also became a personality for the station, hosting numerous broadcasts, interviewing well known public figures and officials, writing and producing for shows, and hosting my own. The purpose for my life was now becoming clearer to me. I may have missed this opportunity, had I continued with that Master's programme. And as for that other radio station which rejected me in the previous year . . .this one was the right fit! If that opportunity was won in my favour, perhaps I would not get to hear many people say to me as they have, how much they've been inspired and blessed through my words and programme.

There are some very important lessons which I learned at this point in my life. It became clear to me that a lack of immediate success or favourable results does not mean you are on the wrong path. It could simply mean that there is more work to be done, perhaps a need for further training. For those of us who identify as Christians, this training is often learning how to trust God. Do not give up because you are not immediately successful. Evaluate where you are, what you have learned and seek to move forward. Finally, perhaps the most profound lesson learned throughout this season is, God always gives us His best even if it means using a prison experience to get us there.

Dream Girl Reflection Section

*How do you feel about the direction in which your life is going?

*What would you change?

Talking to God About - My Purpose

Prayer 4

Father, I know that You have a purpose for me (Psalm 138:8)- it is greater than even I can imagine.

I admit that sometimes I'm not patient about seeing Your work unfold in my life. Lord I grow disheartened when I don't see You answering my prayers, but now I see that like Joseph, You haven't forgotten about me (Ps.139:1-3,7-10). Your great plan for my life is in place, even in the midst of unfavourable circumstances (Job. 42:2).

Teach me to be patient on this journey to fulfilling my dreams.

I know that You give good gifts to your children (Ja. 1:17).

I receive what You have in store for me. I know this situation will turn out for my good, just like Joseph's. Thank You Lord. Amen.

PART TWO

RELEASING LIMITATIONS

~

There's often no way you can look into the
game of life and determine whether or not
you'll get that big break tomorrow or whether
it will take another week, month, year or even
longer. But it will come.

~

Zig Ziglar

5

Goodbye Insecurities

It's sweet- getting to the place you dreamed of, doing the things you always wanted, meeting the people you never imagined you would! Life can take you by surprise at any moment. Like Joseph one moment you're in prison, the next you're in a palace. The good surprises you'll savour for the rest of your life. There also comes a time when you've reached atop the mountain of your dream, and you begin to ask "is there more?" I've been in that place before, and the truth is, even when you've reached a peak, there is always more. However, I've learned too that in the right season, "more" offers you full satisfaction and peace of mind. But in the wrong timing, it can be a source of great discomfort. I've been on both sides of the fence.

After eight months at my first job in radio, I asked myself "is there more?" There certainly is, I reasoned. It was like being at the tip of an iceberg, and wanting to dig deeper. To be a reputable and respected journalist long remained my number one career goal, so when the opportunity came to prove what I was made of, I eagerly took it. Someone very close to me, who knew of my abilities and believed in my potential, tipped me off on a job opening at a state-run media house and encouraged me to apply there. I felt there was greater and went after it. A long period elapsed between the time of my application, a call for assessment, and subsequently an interview. It was two months to be exact. I remained very prayerful throughout this time, listening to hear what the Lord had to say about this move. I became really anxious at some points because I did not receive any indication that my application was successful. I wanted the dream really bad. But when I got it, believe it or not, I was not fully satisfied.

No Need to Prove

New beginnings are almost always nerve-wrecking. With the solid foundation received in my previous position, I was fully ready for all this job would throw at me. My game face was on! I took all my assignments head on, giving them my best shot. There were a few kinks here and there, but as the weeks and months went by I established myself as a valuable team member. That's what was happening on the outside. Inside, it was a totally different scene. There was a void somewhere. I did not feel as I thought I would - happy, joyful, excited. Instead, I was sad. Here I was, at "my dream job", but not enjoying it. Still, I remained grateful and valuable to my new environment; after all, no one was to be blamed for how I was feeling. In the midst of this, I was battling a storm in another area of my life- a broken relationship. It was a bitter period emotionally but I fought to get myself into a positive place.

All of them-
my insecurities,
were lies

When I was really able to fully focus at work, insecurities came knocking at my door. *Was I good enough? Did I measure up? Does anyone recognise my talent? Am I being overlooked?* My mind started measuring myself against other employees, and a plethora of questions concerning my talent began to overwhelm me. Although I knew better and tried to block these mental assaults, they seemed to have found a small place to thrive. I started feeling low on occasions when I wasn't asked to do certain assignments, believing somehow I didn't measure up and that's why I wasn't asked. What was I lacking? The insecurities within me grew. Perhaps I should try doing some things like the others? I needed something to set me apart, I concluded. I hurled numerous criticisms toward myself, until I reached a place of discontent. It was here an important realisation hit- trying to be like the others was not working for me.

Let It Go, It's Not Worth You

I've struggled with a lot of insecurities throughout my life - how I looked, my talents, intellect and so on. Perhaps it's the same for many other young women, maybe even you. As it concerns my career, there was a desire to be out in front and be recognised for what I was doing. I had grown up believing you ought always to be on top. It is only at this stage in my life, I began confronting those ideas. All of them- my insecurities, were lies. Success it seems, always stirs an ant's nest which was buried before. The same insecurities that lead me to earlier start a Master's programme which I had no true need for, re-emerged.

One day, in an effort to confront myself with great honesty,

I sat down and created a list of lies I'd believed about where I was and my abilities, and then truths needed to replace them.

The desire to get ahead-
out of feeling insecure,
can lead you off-track
the very destiny
you were created for

One such truth, which I began to realise with the help of a mentor, is that I was indeed already quite successful. Within a year I had climbed up a ladder which had taken many others a much longer time. I was learning new things, and growing professionally- there was no need to be insecure about my talent; nor jealous of the growth which others too were experiencing in their careers.

The deeper I looked within myself, the more I saw that insecurity played a role in leaving my previous job. There was a desire to prove to myself that I had the abilities to make it even farther in the aggressive media world. I wanted more and I pushed myself toward it. And while there's absolutely nothing wrong with this; I've learned too that if one is not careful, the desire to get ahead- out of feeling insecure - can lead you off-track the very destiny you were created for. Coupled with that, when you are trying to be someone else, you are not giving permission for the gifts and talents which make you unique, to truly come out and be used. When I realised these things I began to speak the truth to myself. I started embracing me, appreciating how far I'd come in a greater way, and that lead me to finally enjoy my job. From this point I was truly able to move into my destiny.

This job was an amazing opportunity. I met with a number of outstanding professionals in the field, talked with government officials, and worked with some of the biggest names in various industries. Not to mention, each week, my voice could be heard on broadcasts across more than twenty radio stations islandwide. My industry skills were also significantly boosted, and I became much more confident about my abilities. Furthermore, it helped me put into perspective what I really wanted in a career. That's why I later decided to leave and head to the place connected with my destiny. There was something which I had started, and needed to complete.

Dream Girl Reflection Section

In the first column of the table below write down the lies which you've believed about yourself, and in the second, truths to replace them with. An example is done for you.

Lies to Dismiss	Truths to Embrace
I am not good enough	I am talented and more than enough

Talking to God About - My Insecurities

Prayer 5

Lord, I doubt my abilities many times. Sometimes I feel as if I'm not good enough or I haven't succeeded enough.

Sometimes I feel that I do not qualify for certain things.

Lord, this moment as I pray to You, I am ready to throw away these negative thoughts about myself, and every feeling of insecurity.

Change my thinking Lord. Help me to accept what You say about me (Isaiah 43:4). Thank You Lord for hearing me. Amen.

6

Making the Right Moves

As a young Christian woman, my life's decisions are woven with my faith. I live by including God in my plans and consulting Him on the way to go. So, when a managerial position at my former job opened up - I knew that was His way of calling me back to where I needed to make a great impact. It was not enough for me to just receive a pay cheque at the end of each month. Instead, it mattered most that I was transforming people's lives with my gifts. Too deep for a twenty-something year old? No, I don't think so. In fact, these are the years to begin building a life legacy; I wanted mine to be built on impact, not image. Long before the position opened up, I knew I'd find myself back at the place where this all started. How I'd get back there is what I did not know. I could not see which road I'd be travelling on to get there, yet I knew it was my destination. How did I know? There was a longing inside me, more than just the average feeling of missing a place. It was a need to complete a mission- to use my strengths in an area where they were needed. As destiny would have it, I was eyed for the position. Within a short time all the right discussions concerning my employment took place. I accepted the offer. It was like the biblical event of the Red Sea parting- everything lined up for me to walk into this new opportunity. The closer I got to my starting date, the more enthused I was. After some time, I was back at my former workplace in an entirely new position, and at a much higher level might I add. Here, I had the opportunity to utilize many of my skills in creating content for radio. It also gave me a seat from which I could present and approve ideas on how to use resources, build employees, strengthen partnerships and more.

My natural leadership abilities were in full gear with this position. Not only was I leading a team, but also adding value to my team members. In addition, I continued being a presenter, producer and personality. This was way more than what I'd dreamed of or planned for, but even more importantly- I was already prepared. Not only were my industry skills well-honed to take on management work, but my heart had been humbled so that I could see my gifts were not just for my own use, but to enhance and uplift others as well.

Tap Into Your Best

When you become connected with your destiny, good, in fact, great things happen. That's because your natural gifts are given the room to flow and grow. No longer do you have to be overly concerned with things that you're not good at- you can focus on what you instinctively do well. Once I settled into my new post, whatever I put my hands, heart and mind to became a success. The excitement and drive which I found caused me to give each task one hundred and fifty per cent. I did more than needed and even gave myself new projects to tackle; each one yielding better results than the first. My personal fulfilment level found new heights. It was a joy to finally be where I wanted.

Giving my best came once the strengths I possessed were being fully embraced, and as others relied upon me for advice on how to tap into their own skills. I saw myself grow in tremendous ways over the course of time. My aim was not just to hold down another job; rather it was to propel my environment to reach its optimal in every imaginable way. One thing which I became even better at was giving

---

When you become connected with your destiny, great things happen

---

feedback. Note I did not say overly criticising. If I might say so myself, I believe I was a balanced manager.

Ever since tapping into my personality, I've realised an innate propensity to help others get to where they need to be. Thus, a big part of me sees the potential in others, and this ability helps me to spur them on to greatness. Each team member I worked with received some piece of advice to help hone their skills. I got this done in several ways. First I caused my colleagues to see that they were valuable to various processes at work, whether they were major projects or regular day-to-day tasks. I've learned that valuing people does a whole lot.

When people know they are valued, you will never have to force them to perform. They will give of themselves out of their own desires. Second, I challenged my colleagues to put their best foot forward on each task, to give more than expected, to challenge their skill level and discover new possibilities for themselves. Doing all of this required me to do something very important- that is, put myself was truly an enriching time in my professional life. Many persons with whom I've worked have been very thankful for my input in their development. Others may not have shown their gratitude externally or directly to me, but being able to see them succeeding has truly been satisfying. Being my best was never just about me, it was about the communities to which I belonged; helping them see their own true worth and capabilities.

Dream Girl Reflection Section

* What's 'the right move' that you need to make at this time in your life?

* Think of the last 'major move' you've made over the last six months to a year. How have you grown since?

Talking to God About - Making the Right Moves

Prayer 6

Lord I'm grateful for every opportunity You've made possible for me. Thank You for going before me and opening doors which I could not on my own (Ps. 75:6). You have done marvellous things in my life and for that I give You praise. Lord I know that my professional life and interests are important to You because You care for every area of my being (1 Peter 5:7; Ps. 139:5). Use me to help others unlock their purpose. Cause me to continue showing how excellent You are, by giving my best and being a blessing unto others. Amen

7

Be Content With Who You Are

I didn't always love every stage of my career. Some stages were quite uncomfortable- like being un-established, your work unknown. At this point you can definitely start feeling like "a nobody". For a very long time, it was my desire to be like many of those other media personalities I admired. *I wish I had a career like hers.... she's so well-liked and in the spotlight...what about me? I can do those very same things and even better...why am I not the one up on that stage...why am I not the one receiving that award...why didn't I get that call? Why? Why? Why?* These questions have plagued me at one point or the other.

Isn't it true that we often want what others have without even knowing their story? We even neglect our own talents as we spend time envying others. Focusing too much on what others have and not on how you can develop your own skills, is a huge distraction. We usually perceive that the grass is greener on the other side, but I'd like to let you know that there is no gain in longing for what others have, or in envying them for where they are in their careers. On the contrary, there is much fulfilment in watching your own growth and appreciating every step of your journey.

Own Your Talent

It can be painful working with someone who is not confident in their talent. Are you confident about yours? As recent as six months before starting this book, I had some doubt in mine. That was due to some of the insecurities I highlighted above and in previous chapters. When you don't know what you have, you'll never value it, and chances are you'll never reap its benefits.

As soon as I started owning my talents and passions I became better at them and realised there were countless opportunities for their use. Upon starting out in radio, I never imagined becoming a personality. Sure it was one of those things I always wanted to do, but not one that I would exactly put myself forward for. At the time, my passion was in the areas news planning, production and presenting so I focused much of my energy in that direction, never realising there was much more I could do. Then an opportunity came. I was working as Producer on a live broadcast surrounding a sensitive national issue- one of regional interest. It so happened that the original presenter was to be out for a week and all eyes fell on me to take on that task. I was absolutely nervous. Who mentioned that I could do this?? Well, I did do "it" for several days. With a pounding heart in chest, I donned my headset, with microphone in hand and set out on the course laid out for me. I recall on each occasion experiencing a burst of excitement and energy for on-location presenting, a skill which I did not pay much attention to prior to this turn of events.

> *there is much fulfilment in watching your own growth and appreciating every step of your journey*

This came very naturally for me, and while it was an experience of being on pins and needles (I was broadcasting from a live protest) it showed me my own potential and solidified my skills in the minds of others. I had fun while presenting as I connected with listeners. And guess what? I spoke my way right into their hearts. From then I remained a top pick for the station's broadcasts -I've done so many it's hard to count. My talent was unleashed and I embraced it. Each broadcast was an opportunity for me to become better at this art. As I refined my skills the opportunities for on-air presenting outside of my core function as News Editor and Presenter increased. I covered national events, commemorative services, renowned gospel events, interviewed national leaders and so much more. This new area of my job had become a joy to me!

On this journey of owning my talent, one shining

Unless you come to terms with your own potential and tap into it, you will never possess that confidence needed for the next level

---

moment was meeting a popular radio and television broadcaster who was thrilled when I mentioned my name. To my astonishment she had already known about me, and gave high commendations which I did not expect to receive! That moment meant so much to me, especially because in this field it can be difficult to stand out among others who maintain a high standard of excellence. I'm glad someone else, who had gone farther in the industry and was so much more successful, could acknowledge what I already knew to be true. This gave me an extra pep in my step! Unless you come to terms with your own potential and tap into it, you will never possess that confidence needed for the next level. For years I was told that I had an excellent speaking voice and I knew deep down I had a career and passion connected to it. I'm glad that when the opportunities arose for me to be connected with my passions, I also rose to the occasion and delivered what I knew was within me.

What's your passion? Are you owning it, and have you been benefiting from it? In what area are you hoping to make a mark? Start embracing who you are and what you have today. Even in an area where you may have been for a long time, there is always more to learn. Once you embrace this, your growth process will be filled with less trepidation and become rewarding.

Make Your Mark

Following my start in radio, word on my talent could hardly be hid. I'd grown somewhat of a fan base from persons in all age groups. On many occasions when I said my name in public or over the phone, I got a second look, a smile, animated conversation and a plethora of heartfelt commendations. People often said, "you've blessed me in so many ways", "I listen to you all the time", "your voice is lovely - keep up the good work". Compliments such as those served to remind me that I did take the right path and my hard work was aimed in the right direction.

In my profession, I've often been challenged to "be more creative" or "come up with something new". I take these opportunities to push myself and explore my talent or my team-mates' in innovative ways. The result has always been excellence because I strive to move away from mediocrity.

In the creative industries, it is often said that you are as good as your last piece of work. That means, what you have done most recently, not the month or year before, is the benchmark against which you are being measured. How did that look for me on my job? Well for starters, each month I was responsible for spear-heading an on-air campaign to highlight a particular focus. Apart from keeping relevant, I had to tap into the minds of listeners and ask myself "what information do they need to hear most right now?" Once I answered that question, the rest was history and my creative juices immediately started flowing.

Polish Yourself

You are a gem. You must embrace this in order to bring out the best in yourself. Every once in a while it is good to remind yourself of how far you've come, how much you've grown and the impact you've made. Of course this is not an invitation to let arrogance steal your warmth.

When you know and reveal your true worth by investing yourself in what makes you feel empowered, the whole world will see it.

Dream Girl Reflection Section

 * How content are you with your current abilities?

A. Mostly content

B. Never content

C. A little content

 * How often do I doubt my abilities?

A. Each time I'm asked to do something

B. Most occasions

C. Every few occasions

After providing your own answers, ask a friend these questions concerning you then share what you both have noticed.

Talking to God About - Being Content in Who I am

Prayer 7

Lord You have made me in a unique way.

I have gifts, talents and strengths which You have given unto me for my purpose. Help me to experience fulfillment in the way You have designed my abilities. Lord, cause me not to envy others. Help me to be grateful for the talents I already have (Matt. 14:19-23). Cause me to appreciate where I am on this journey of pursuing my dreams. Amen

8

An Essential Characteristic

With hard work anyone can get to the places they've dreamed. As is often said however, it takes character to keep you there. I find that many young professionals- those in my age group and even younger, who are significantly talented in some area neglect holding to this advice. As a result, working with them is a constant pain, because their attitudes leave much to be desired. I'd like to warn you- avoid getting to this place. Aptitude will surely get you great jobs and big breaks, but attitude will colour your experience and that's what people remember you by.

Show Up, But Don't Show Off

Humility is key in every area of life. Always has been and always will be. Period. Success is unpalatable without humility. You need it in order to go farther. No one likes celebrating a push-over or an arrogant individual.

***Success
is unpalatable without
humility.
You need it in order to go
farther***

Across the spectrum of my work experiences, I've encountered a number of figures in various positions, who exemplified the lack of humility which irked fellow employees, and hurt the business image. In all cases, I witnessed a colossal fall of some sort, directly connected with a foul attitude. I've even had to supervise such individuals. On the level of both supervisor and fellow employee, it's been a sore sight.

One such employee I formerly supervised, I'll call her Samantha, holds firmly in my memory. When I think of uncommon aptitude which gets the job done, Samantha comes to mind. When I also think of selfishness and a proud attitude which impacts employee relations, she also comes to mind. I often had a hard time relating with her. Although she was a highly skilled employee, working alongside her was troublesome. From my very keen observation, it seemed Samantha made it her point of duty to push the limits around her- breaking office procedures and codes of conduct, disrespecting senior employees and the list went on. She often displayed very little team spirit and eventually received a number of suspensions on her record.

No amount of one-on-one talks seemed to really get through to her. The most disconcerting part about working with Samantha was, only her attitude hindered her from making a greater impact. On more than one occasion, she could have received a promotion; however with the profile mentioned before, this never came into being.

What is the lesson here? While talent and skill show that you know what to do, your attitude determines how you impact your environment and those within it, especially when you've tasted success. The right attitude will draw others toward you. The wrong one does nothing but drive people away. When the latter happens, it is unlikely that you'll receive the guidance needed for the steps ahead of you. This could lead to you turning away the people whose help you may need the most.

Dream Girl Reflection Section

*How important do you feel humility is to your character and success?
A. A little important
B. Highly important
C. Of no importance at all

*Do you bear any similarity to the persona described in this chapter?
A. Strikingly similar, I'm concerned
B. Not even close, quite the opposite
C. A bit, definitely an area to work on

After providing your own answers, ask a friend these questions concerning you then share what you both have noticed.

Talking to God About - My Characterstics

Prayer 8

Lord, Your word tells me that You resist the proud,
but show favour to the humble (Ja. 4:6).
As I experience success, cause me to walk in humility.
Help me not to be arogant.
Keep me in Your grace.
Teach me how to work along with others.
Cause my character to be an example to others.
If ever my success becomes a chip on my shoulder,
please point me instead to the way that is Yours.
Remind me that it is Your strength which
enables me to do well (Phil. 4:13). Amen

9

Your Dream Team

Dreaming alone can only take you so far. The journey to realising your dreams is much more rewarding when there are people around to inspire, encourage and support you. I call them your dream team. Now, I'm not talking about the regular 'pat on the back' kind of support which is usually characteristic of family and friends. While that's certainly to be appreciated, your dream team members offer so much more. With them impossibilities are made possible, and your biggest dreams can become reality as a result of their contributions. Many of my accomplishments would not have been possible without my very own dream team. They were there to guide me, support my decision-making and even say if they thought I was making a wrong move. My dream team members and I have not always shared the same opinions or conclusions, but they are sincerest in their feelings toward me and want very much to see my success. They provide balance to my visions and increase my confidence, helping me believe I can make it. As you go after your vision these are the people you need throughout the seasons of life- whether you're being highly productive, or desperately need some inspiration.

Matches Made in Heaven

Husbands and wives are not the only people whom God ordains for relationship. He does so too with mentors or role models, and being the wise God He is, they always appear at the appointed time. Right after completing my first degree, I got the opportunity which helped steer me toward pursuing the media career of which I dreamed.

A freelance Television Producer and Photographer invited me to become her Production Assistant. She had known of my interest in the media industry, and gave me the chance to learn more. That I certainly did. Under her tutelage, the world of video production and photography became open before me. I relished each project on which we worked- from photo shoots to documentaries and weddings. The journey was filled with excitement, hard work and joy. This woman, my very first mentor in the media profession was unselfish in sharing her passion, life and work.

Over the course of our two years working together, she taught me the 'ins and outs' of the media industry, its best practices, and even how to balance a demanding job with family life. Now a few years later, as an established media practitioner I credit much of my intrigue and passion for the media arts to her.

realising your dreams
is much more rewarding
when there are people
around to inspire,
encourage and support
you

She ignited in me an eagerness to learn, as well as helped me develop the diligence to see excellent results. Because of her I hold this desire to own a production company as she does, and to be the absolute best at what I do. This is one of the most valuable mentoring relationships I've experienced in my life. I wouldn't trade it for anything. Today I can call upon this special woman to give me advice on career moves, projects or just about any other area of life. She has become so much more than just a mentor to me, she is a sister and will always be part of my dream team.

At another crossroad in my life, I met another member of my dream team. This relationship too, I've continued to cherish. After working in Video and Photography for two years, I moved into Radio. It was in this field that I came across this member of my dream team- a gifted radio personality and media manager. Like my previous mentor, we share an immense passion for the work that we do. This has lead to us collaborating in a number of areas: producing radio shows, creating content, doing major or minor projects and so much more. I'd found another treasure who invested in me wholescale.

This mentor saw in me great talent and skill which may have otherwise gone untapped. He provided me with opportunities to hone my abilities even in the midst of anxiety and fear, while teaching me how to be balanced in the pursuit of my career. With his guidance, I became involved in every aspect of radio production, media planning and management. Today much of the very deep knowledge I have of radio, was gained through this remarkable figure. My life and dreams wouldn't be the same without his very invaluable input.

The Right Fit

Encountering your dream team members is a life-altering

experience. Through these persons you realise more potential in yourself than on your own could have ever discovered. That's why it is important that you know how to recognise these persons when they do enter your life. You'll observe that they:

•*Provide unwavering support regardless of what's happening in life.*

•*Are never burdened by your zeal to learn more; rather they pour into you what they know.*

•*Encourage you to take calculated risks in line with your dream.*

•*Challenge you to grow, gain new experiences and broaden your knowledge base.*

•*Consistently encourage you to work toward your vision.*

If you haven't already, I fervently hope that you'll meet your dream team members very soon. When you do encounter them, do not fear being vulnerable and open about your vision. You'll realise it comes natural to share with them. Make time to sit at their feet and learn as much as you can for the journey you're on. Be humble about the stage where you're at, and take the necessary advice while enjoying the experience of this journey. I assure you, these

Dream Girl Reflection Section

*Can you identify in your life the dream team members I've described in this chapter?

*In what ways have their investments helped you toward pursuing your dreams?

Talking to God About - My Dream Team

Prayer 9

Lord I know that I cannot make it on this journey all by myself.
As I pursue my dreams, I need the help of others whom You will use
to guide and direct me toward achieving my goals (Prov. 11:14;Ecc. 4:9)
Show me who these people are.
Connect me with them in the right time.
Cause me to nurture these relationships and learn from them.
May I listen to their wisdom (Prov. 13:20) and experience
growth as I interact with them (Prov. 27:17). Thank You for blessing
me with people who inspire me to pursue my dreams. Amen

10

Never Stop Dreaming

So what's next for you? I'm sure you've heard this question being asked during celebrity interviews. What is the most common response which you've heard? I guarantee you that it usually goes something like this- "well right now I'm working on...", "I'm now in the process of ...", "I just started..." What do you notice here? People who have already achieved some kind of success rarely stop in their tracks because they've "done it all". On the contrary, they continue in a forward moving direction- overcoming obstacles, defeating odds and securing greater victories. Sometimes they even delve into fields which they had never previously explored, or returned to a long held childhood dream. Whatever the specific goal, they never stopped dreaming. I now pose that same question to you- what's next? Where are you presently in achieving your goals, and where do you see yourself in the future? Have you stopped working toward a goal because you think there is nothing more you can do? Or are you still inside the blocks? Perhaps you're nowhere near the experiences described throughout this book. Before you dismiss the idea of ever achieving success or going further than where you now are, think about this- who benefits from your lack of progression? No one does- neither yourself nor your environment filled with others around you. On the contrary, when you decide to move forward by allowing yourself to continue dreaming despite what life brings, you most certainly win from that moment. You also win when you reap the tangible benefits of your hard work, and perhaps the greatest win is seeing your actions positively impacting others.

Over the last few years, I've been inspired by persons who after having met significant success just kept going. I am happy to say that my mother is one such person. I have never heard her say that she's given up on something, rather she is always working on the next goal. Most recently just before hitting the big fifty, she graduated from a college diploma programme which has helped to take her to the next level in her career as a Nurse. While many persons her age would dread returning to a classroom, she has done so on multiple occasions, and the results have been phenomenal! She is always looking ahead for opportunities to develop her skills. This woman inspires me so much. At her age she hasn't slowed down on accomplishing her dreams. Rather, she is in full gear working towards being at the top of her profession. If she can do that, what is stopping you or me?

Writing this book has been a dream of mine, and let me tell you- it has not been easy. But as I share my experiences with you, I am continually encouraged, and so I press on. Despite obstacles, I never gave up, and look at the result!

when you decide to move forward
by allowing yourself to continue
dreaming despite what life brings,
you most certainly win from that
moment

Be encouraged. Take that next step! Dream yourself to the next level! Make that move toward a great achievement. Even if you don't have it all mapped out, just take a glimpse at yourself beyond today and record what you see, then go after it! My own response to that aforementioned question posed has numerous responses. I intended it that way, knowing that what I've accomplished so far is not the whole. There is much of my potential still untapped, but I'm making my best effort to get to all the places where my skills and talents are at their optimal. So should you!

Never Stop Discovering

I recently experienced an epiphany which has somehow changed my outlook on life, particularly my career. When I moved to New York to pursue a Master's degree (in Media ofcourse!), my eyes were opened to the varied directions in which my career could go. Thoughts previously far removed began flooding me; options unconsidered were floating in my head. Thus I found myself on a journey, piecing together what my future life could look like. Suddenly came the realisation that I need not limit myself to any one thing! Sure I'd always known I can be anything I want to be, but here's the greatest, and possibly hidden part of that- it doesn't have to be one thing. I can be an Author, Television Producer, PhD Candidate and a Teacher even while running my own production company. It all is possible!

Once I began to embrace this, I looked at going even further into dimensions I had not believed probable for me. Like the saying goes, don't put your eggs in one basket. It is great to have a career goal or direction. In addition to that, remaining open to new possibilities on the journey toward pursuing your dreams, can be highly beneficial. Never stop discovering your potential! There is more inside of you than you can conceive. Never limit your dreams to one time frame- things can happen sooner, as they can later. The possibilities truly are endless.

Stay Motivated

Motivation is like that warm cup of coffee, tea or orange juice which you have in the morning before getting down to business. It wakes you up inside and gives you perspective on getting what you need to do done. The more you have of it, the more you keep going at those tasks you wish to fulfil. If you want to go further with your dreams, you must remain motivated. This is a key part of your success.

Without motivation you are unlikely to stay in the driver's seat of life and gear through everything that comes your way. Consider this- if ever you begin working towards a goal and suddenly sense your energy for that thing shifting, check your motivation level. Do you really believe in what you're doing? Is it your passion? It's best to answer these questions at an early stage, rather than exhausting yourself mentally, emotionally, and physically only to realise you're heading nowhere. If in the affirmative, look at where you may be falling down and redirect yourself into improving this.

or a career change in order to realise what path best suits you. Be mindful too that there will have to be dedicated sacrifices of time and resources in order to reach that fulfilling career path.

Whatever positive move you need to make towards your dream, do it while you have the ability. Gain inspiration towards your achievements and release the limitations holding you back. No matter where in life you are right now, it is imperative for you to know that you can dream, girl!

Dream Girl Reflection Section

* What is the next step in your journey towards realising your dreams?

* How has this book helped you toward that?

Talking to God About - My Dreams (Again)

Prayer 10

Father, Your word says that You will instruct me and
teach me in the way which I should go (Ps. 32:8).
As I puruse my dreams, cause me to remain
open about the plans which You have.
Although I have set goals which I desire to accomplish, I
know that it is You who will bring them to pass (Prov. 19:21).
Lord, I give all of these plans to You.
Bring them about in Your own time and in Your own way,
for Your time and ways are best (Ecc. 3:11).
Keep me from discouragement.
Help me to remain focused even in the midst of challenges.
Cause me to know that You are writing my story,
and You are not through with me yet.
I give You thanks for all You have done for me.
I give You thanks for fulfilling my dreams. Amen

ACKNOWLEDGEMENTS

To my parents, Marvin and Christine, thank you for inspiring me to "dream big", and raising me to be a bold and successful woman. Writing this book was made possible because you have always supported my dreams; I owe very much to you both. Your emotional and financial support even as an adult, has contributed to my success.

To Halthea Latty and Ronn Albert- two of my 'media mentors', how do I fully say thank you? I am very blessed to have experienced your tutelage, and even happier that our relationships moved beyond the 'know how', translating into something purposeful and beautiful.

Odette Baugh, your contribution to the production of this book is invaluable. Dr. Kadian Walters, your love and support over the years has been a tremendous blessing. Thank you for the very thorough and insghtful feedback you offered on the entire project. Gillian Whyte, thank you for the spark of inspiration which you unknowingly provided by publishing your own book, and for sharing your experience.

Savrenee Lee, I cannot forget the countless late nights you stayed up to hear me talk about this book! Orville Perrier, you believed in this long before I mentioned it! People like you are few! Thanks for all the encouragement and prayers. Likewise, Shawana Wright and Alex Young, I am truly grateful for your persistent prayers and encouragement from the day I mentioned this.

My editor, Kyshuri Ranger and cover designer Rounica White, ours have been divine connections. I am amazed at how quickly you both caught this vision! The Lord knew I needed you and sent you both in a timely manner. Thank you both for believing in this and providing the energy to match same.

To my Pastors at Miracle Open Bible Church, I am so very grateful for your years of guidance and encouragement throughout my personal and spiritual development.

I also extend heartfelt gratitude to Belinda Demercado and my intercessory family. Thank you for grounding me in prayer. I love you all.

Many others have thrown their full support behind me while I worked to put this book together. While it is impossible to mention each one of you, please do know that your contributions have been noted.

Finally, to my Lord- the Triune God, may You ever be pleased with the song which my life sings unto You.

ABOUT THE AUTHOR

Kediesha R. Watkis is a graduate of the University of the West Indies, Mona where she earned a Bachelor of Arts degree in Literatures in English and History (Honours).

A few years after graduating, Kediesha launched into the Jamaican media landscape in which she has since enjoyed notable success as a Writer, Presenter and Producer for radio at the corporate and mainstream levels.

She is an avid reader, researcher and lover of the literary, performing, and media arts. Additionally, she is trained in the areas of communication and leadership.

Over the last eight years, Kediesha has served as Youth Leader and Advisor within auxiliary departments of Open Bible Standard Churches of Jamaica (OBSCJ). As part of her leadership, she has spent dedicated time developing and executing programmes aimed at equipping girls and young women with requisite skills for purpose-filled living.

Kediesha is now pursuing graduate studies in Media Arts at Long Island University, New York.

Join the #DreamGirlMovement
and share
your *Dream GIRL Experience!*

Connect via these social media networks
using the handle **@dreamgirlmovement**

Visit www.dreamgirlmovement.com

Author Invitation and Group Book Orders

Kediesha is excited about speaking
at your next youth/women's conference,
small group meeting or seminar!

Please send requests and invitations to
thedreamgirlmovement@gmail.com

Group order information:
Special discounts are available on quantity purchases by youth
ministries, young women's groups, associations, and others.
Place orders by writing to the email address above.

www.ingramcontent.com/pod-product-compliance
Lightning Source LLC
Chambersburg PA
CBHW060948040426
42445CB00011B/1053